PLASTIC C

Plastic Canvas
Bag Holders™

By Debra Arch

Pastel Posies

Size: 5 inches W x 11¼ inches H x 4¼ inches D
(12.7cm x 28.6cm x 10.8cm)
Skill Level: Beginner

Materials

❑ 1 artist-size sheet clear stiff 7-count plastic canvas
❑ 2 sheets white 7-count plastic canvas
❑ Uniek Needloft plastic canvas yarn as listed in color key
❑ 2-inch (5.1cm) gold metal ring
❑ #16 tapestry needle

Stitching Step by Step

Dispenser

1 From clear stiff plastic canvas, cut dispenser front and dispenser top according to graphs. From white plastic canvas, cut base according to graph, and one rectangle 33 holes x 73 holes for dispenser back; base and back will remain unstitched.

2 Stitch top according to graph.

3 Work all horizontal stitches on dispenser front according to graph using a double strand of yarn. Straight Stitch around flower petals using one strand of white yarn.

4 Whipstitch ring to top center edge of white plastic canvas back so that it extends 1 inch (2.5cm) beyond top edge as shown in photo.

Lining

From clear stiff plastic canvas, cut top lining and base lining according to graphs. From white plastic canvas, cut one rectangle 70 holes x 71 holes for front lining and one rectangle 29 holes x 71 holes for back lining. Lining pieces will remain unstitched.

Assembly

1 Using white yarn throughout, Whipstitch side edges of front lining to side edges of back lining.

2 Whipstitch top lining to the upper edge of front and back lining, and bottom lining to lower edge of front and back lining to complete lining.

3 Whipstitch side edges of stitched dispenser front to side edges of dispenser back. Slide lining into dispenser.

4 Whipstitch outer curved edges of dispenser base to outer curved edges at bottom of dispenser.

5 Whipstitch inner curved edges of base and base lining together.

6 Whipstitch through all layers along back straight edges of dispenser back, base and base lining.

7 Whipstitch dispenser top to upper edge of dispenser front and back. Whipstitch top and top lining together around inner opening.

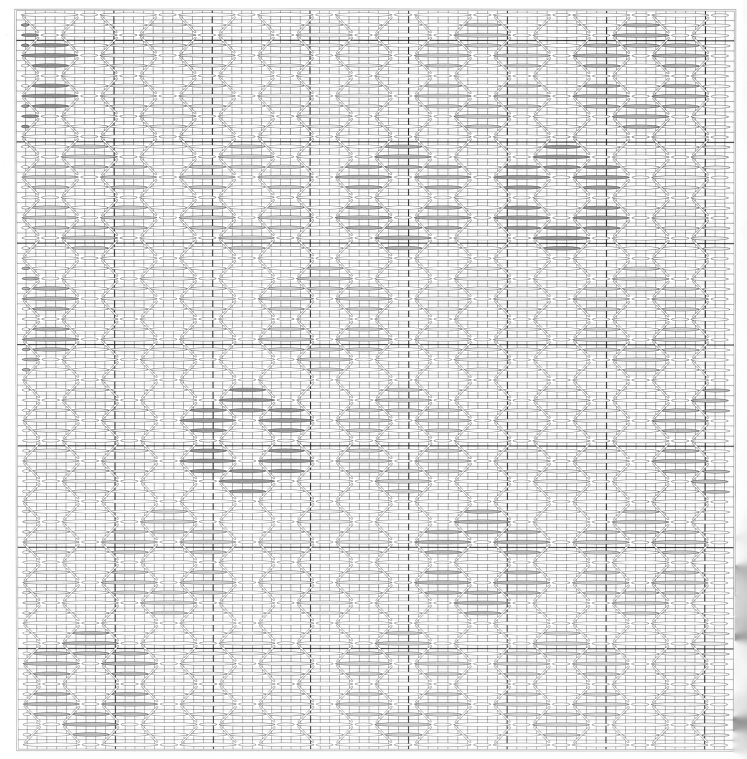

Pastel Posies Dispenser Front
73 holes x 73 holes
Cut 1 from clear stiff

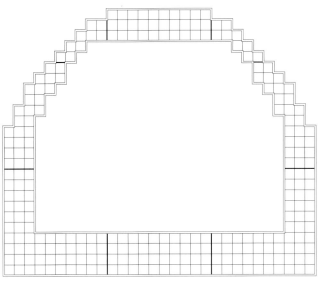

Top Lining
30 holes x 25 holes
For Pastel Posies and Simply Citrus, cut 1 from clear stiff

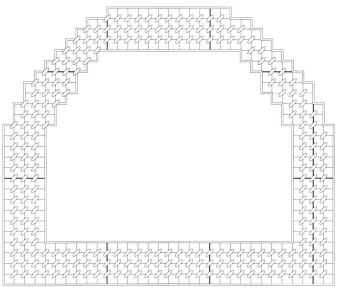

Dispenser Top
32 holes x 26 holes
For Pastel Posies and Simply Citrus, cut 1 from clear stiff
For Simply Citrus, substitute sandstone yarn for white

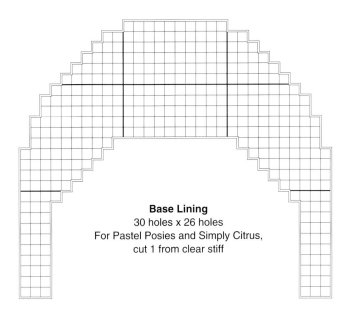

Base Lining
30 holes x 26 holes
For Pastel Posies and Simply Citrus,
cut 1 from clear stiff

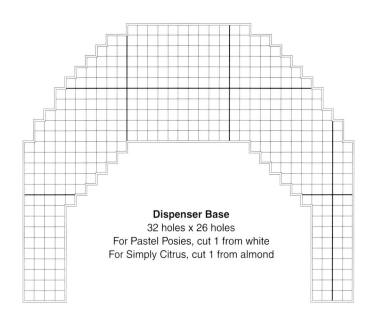

Dispenser Base
32 holes x 26 holes
For Pastel Posies, cut 1 from white
For Simply Citrus, cut 1 from almond

COLOR KEY	
Yards	**Plastic Canvas Yarn**
20 (18.3m)	▩ Tangerine #11
20 (18.3m)	☐ Lemon #20
20 (18.3m)	▧ Fern #23
20 (18.3m)	☐ Baby blue #36
140 (128m)	☐ White #41
20 (18.3m)	▨ Orchid #44
12 (11m)	▨ Lilac #45
	⁄ White #41 Straight Stitch

Color numbers given are for Uniek Needloft
plastic canvas yarn.

Beach Bounty

Size: 6¾ inches in diameter x 6⅝ inches H
(17.2cm x 16.8cm)

Skill Level: Beginner

Materials

❏ 1 artist-size sheet clear 7-count plastic canvas
❏ 9-inch (22.9cm) QuickShape plastic canvas circle from Uniek
❏ Uniek Needloft plastic canvas yarn as listed in color key
❏ Kreinik ⅛-inch (3mm) metallic ribbon as listed in color key
❏ Sulyn Industries Mainstays Crafts glass E beads:
    149 pearl
    37 dark green
❏ Needles: #16 tapestry, sewing needle
❏ White sewing thread
❏ Clean, empty 34½-ounce metal coffee can with lid
❏ White spray paint (optional)
❏ Hot-glue gun

Project Note

Work with a double strand of bright blue plastic canvas yarn when stitching canister side. Work with a single strand when stitching canister top.

Stitching Step by Step

1 Cut one canister side, two shells, two starfish and three sea horses from 7-count plastic canvas according to graphs. Cut one canister top from the 9-inch (22.9cm) plastic canvas circle.

2 Stitch canister side, top, shells, starfish and sea horses according to graphs, filling in uncoded areas on shells and starfish with star green metallic ribbon.

3 Using white yarn throughout, work Straight Stitches on shells; Overcast shells and starfish. Using pearl metallic ribbon, Overcast sea horses. Using bright blue yarn, Overcast center opening in canister top.

4 Using sewing needle and white thread through step 5, attach dark green E beads to shells, starfish and sea horses where indicated by red dots on graphs.

5 Attach pearl E beads to canister side and top where indicated by gold dots on graphs.

6 Form three 1¼-inch (3.2cm) double-loop bows from star green metallic ribbon. Hot-glue a bow to the neck of each sea horse where indicated by blue dot on graph.

Assembly

1 Bend canister side into a ring. Using bright blue yarn through step 2, Whipstitch short ends together.

2 Whipstitch canister top to upper edge of canister side; Overcast lower edge.

3 Hot-glue shells, starfish and sea horses to canister side as shown in photo.

Finishing

1 Spray coffee can white, if desired. Let dry.

2 Using pattern provided, cut a 4-inch (10.2cm) circle from center of plastic coffee-can lid.

3 Fill coffee can with plastic bags. Place lid on can. Slide stitched cover over can.

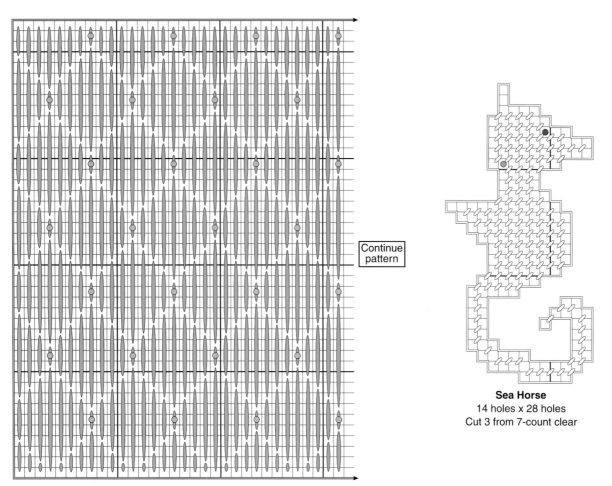

Beach Bounty Canister Side
136 holes x 43 holes
Cut 1 from 7-count clear

Continue pattern

Sea Horse
14 holes x 28 holes
Cut 3 from 7-count clear

COLOR KEY

Yards	Plastic Canvas Yarn
140 (128m)	▦ Bright blue #60
7 (6.4m)	⟋ White #41 Overcast and Straight Stitch
	¹/₈-Inch Metallic Ribbon
30 (27.4m)	☐ Pearl #032
30 (27.4m)	Uncoded areas are star green #9194 Continental Stitches
	◉ Attach pearl E bead
	● Attach dark green E bead
	◉ Attach bow

Color numbers given are for Uniek Needloft plastic canvas yarn and Kreinik ¹/₈-inch metallic ribbon.

4-Inch Circle
Cut 1 from center of plastic coffee-can lid for
Beach Bounty and Butterfly Wing Bling

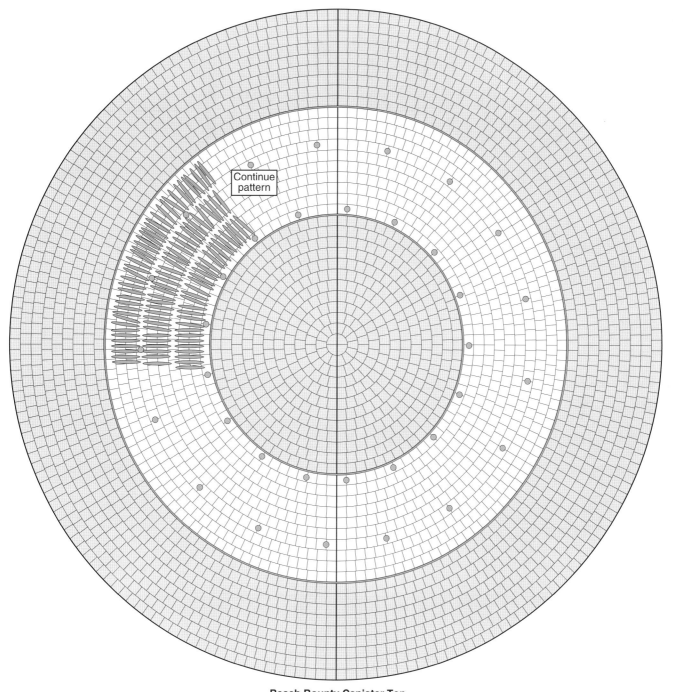

Continue pattern

Beach Bounty Canister Top
Cut 1 from 9-inch plastic canvas circle, cutting away gray areas

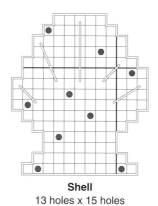

Shell
13 holes x 15 holes
Cut 2 from 7-count clear

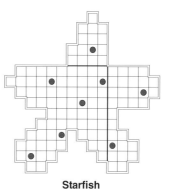

Starfish
15 holes x 15 holes
Cut 2 from 7-count clear

Radiant Rooster

Size: 5¼ inches W x 12 inches H x 4¼ inches D
(13.3cm x 30.5cm x 10.8cm)
Skill Level: Beginner

Materials

- ❑ Clear stiff 7-count plastic canvas:
    2 artist-size sheets
    2 regular-size sheets
- ❑ Uniek Needloft plastic canvas yarn as listed in color key
- ❑ Kreinik ⅛-inch (3mm) metallic ribbon as listed in color key
- ❑ 2-inch (5.1cm) gold metal ring
- ❑ ⁷⁄₁₆-inch (1.1cm) black dome button
- ❑ Needles: #16 tapestry, sewing needle
- ❑ Black thread
- ❑ Hot-glue gun

Stitching Step by Step

Project Note

Work with a single strand of yarn unless otherwise instructed.

Rooster Dispenser

1 Cut two rooster bodies, one dispenser front, one wing, one dispenser top and one dispenser base from plastic canvas according to graphs. One body will remain unstitched for backing.

2 Using sandstone yarn, stitch top and base according to graphs.

3 Using 2 strands of sandstone yarn and 1 strand burgundy metallic ribbon, stitch one body, dispenser front and wing according to graphs, noting that a portion of the body remains unstitched.

4 When background stitching is complete, Straight Stitch crosses on body and dispenser front with black yarn. Straight Stitch crosses on wing with burgundy metallic ribbon. Overcast wing using black yarn.

5 Using needle and thread, stitch button to rooster for eye where indicated by yellow dot on graph.

6 Using sandstone yarn, Whipstitch ring to top center edge of *unstitched* rooster body so that it extends 1 inch (2.5cm) beyond top edge as shown in photo.

Lining

Cut top, base, front and back lining pieces from plastic canvas according to graphs; they will remain unstitched.

Assembly

1 Using sandstone yarn through step 2, Whipstitch side edges of front lining to side edges of back lining.

2 Whipstitch top lining to top edges and bottom lining to bottom edges to complete lining.

3 Referring to photo and using black and sandstone yarn according to graphs, Whipstitch side edges of stitched dispenser front to stitched rooster body in areas between red dots. Slide lining into dispenser.

4 *Using sandstone yarn, Whipstitch stitched top to dispenser front:* Beginning at left arrow on top edge of rooster body graph and working to the left, Whipstitch back straight edge of top to rooster body. Continue Whipstitching top around curved edge of dispenser front and across back straight edge, stopping at right arrow. *Note: Straight edges of top and rooster body between neck and tail remain unstitched for now.*

5 Using sandstone yarn through step 7, Whipstitch top and top lining together around inner opening.

6 Whipstitch outer curved edges of base to outer curved edges at bottom of dispenser.

7 Holding unstitched backing against rooster body, Whipstitch through all layers across straight edge at back of base.

8 Using black yarn, Whipstitch backing to rooster, working through all layers along straight edge of top between neck and tail.

9 Using sandstone yarn, Whipstitch base to base lining around inner opening.

10 Hot-glue wing to front of dispenser as shown in photo.

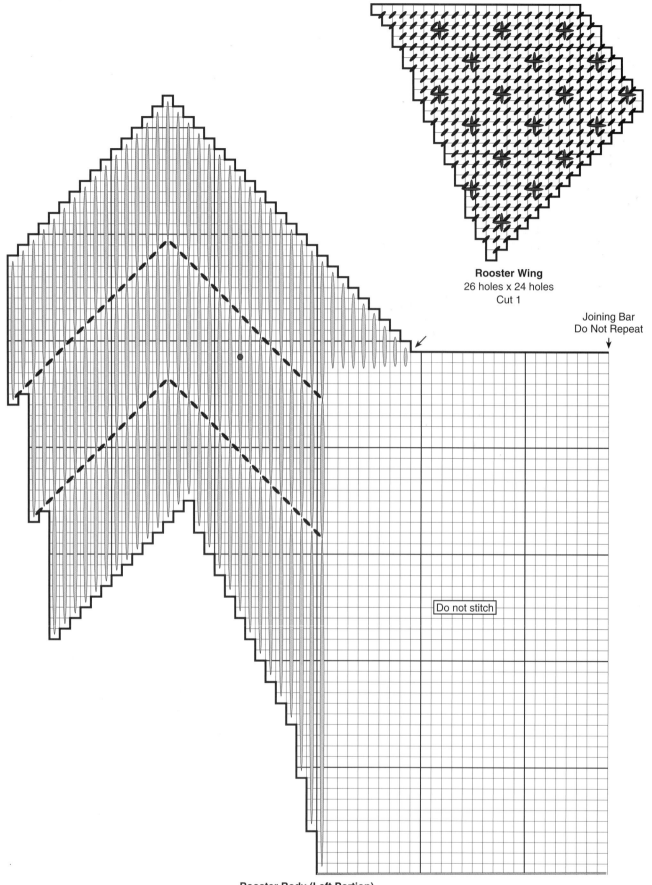

Rooster Wing
26 holes x 24 holes
Cut 1

Joining Bar
Do Not Repeat

Do not stitch

Rooster Body (Left Portion)
92 holes x 79 holes
Join with right portion before cutting as 1 piece
Cut 2, stitch 1

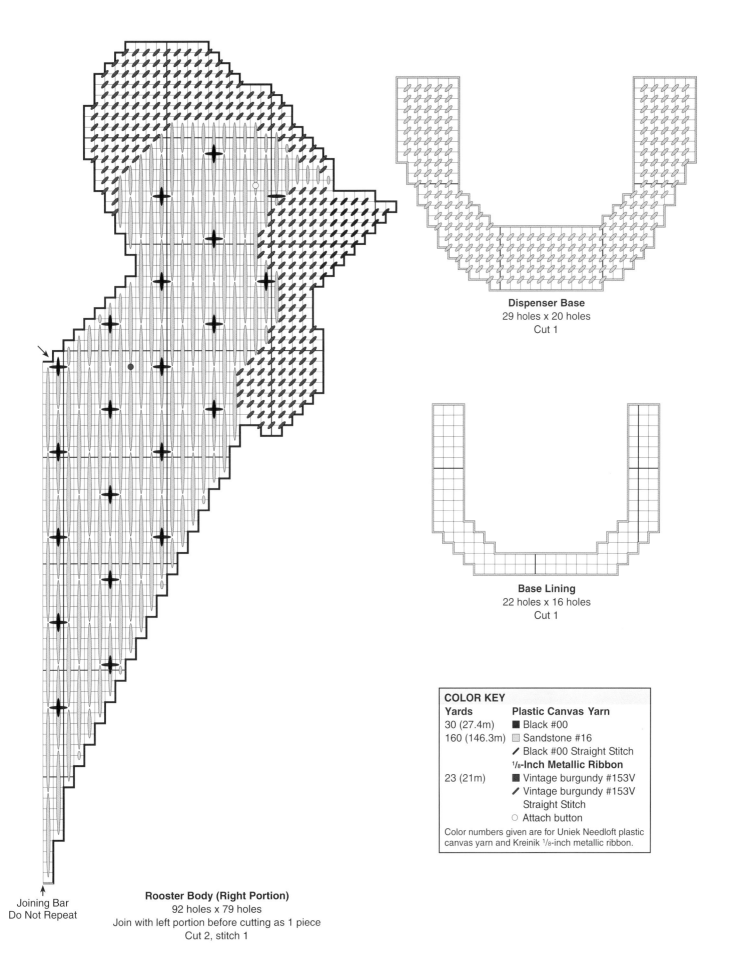

Dispenser Base
29 holes x 20 holes
Cut 1

Base Lining
22 holes x 16 holes
Cut 1

COLOR KEY

Yards	Plastic Canvas Yarn
30 (27.4m)	■ Black #00
160 (146.3m)	☐ Sandstone #16
	╱ Black #00 Straight Stitch
	⅛-Inch Metallic Ribbon
23 (21m)	■ Vintage burgundy #153V
	╱ Vintage burgundy #153V Straight Stitch
	○ Attach button

Color numbers given are for Uniek Needloft plastic canvas yarn and Kreinik ⅛-inch metallic ribbon.

Joining Bar
Do Not Repeat

Rooster Body (Right Portion)
92 holes x 79 holes
Join with left portion before cutting as 1 piece
Cut 2, stitch 1

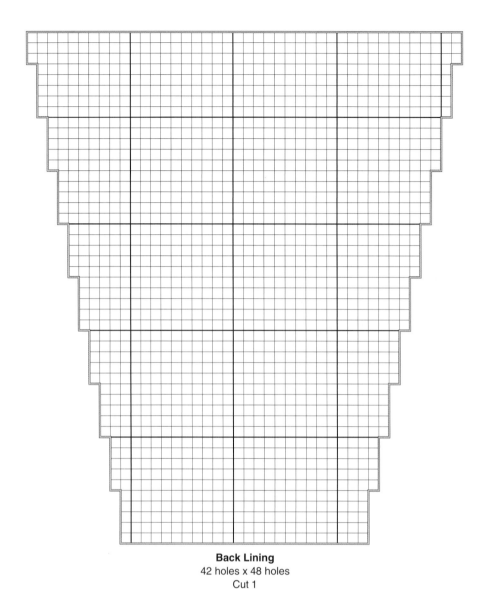

Back Lining
42 holes x 48 holes
Cut 1

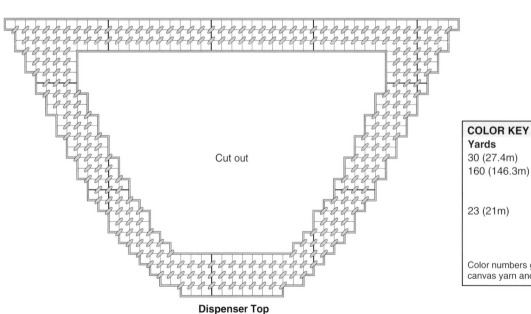

Cut out

Dispenser Top
44 holes x 26 holes
Cut 1

COLOR KEY		
Yards	**Plastic Canvas Yarn**	
30 (27.4m)	■	Black #00
160 (146.3m)	▨	Sandstone #16
	╱	Black #00 Straight Stitch
	1/8-Inch Metallic Ribbon	
23 (21m)	■	Vintage burgundy #153V
	╱	Vintage burgundy #153V Straight Stitch
	○	Attach button

Color numbers given are for Uniek Needloft plastic canvas yarn and Kreinik 1/8-inch metallic ribbon.

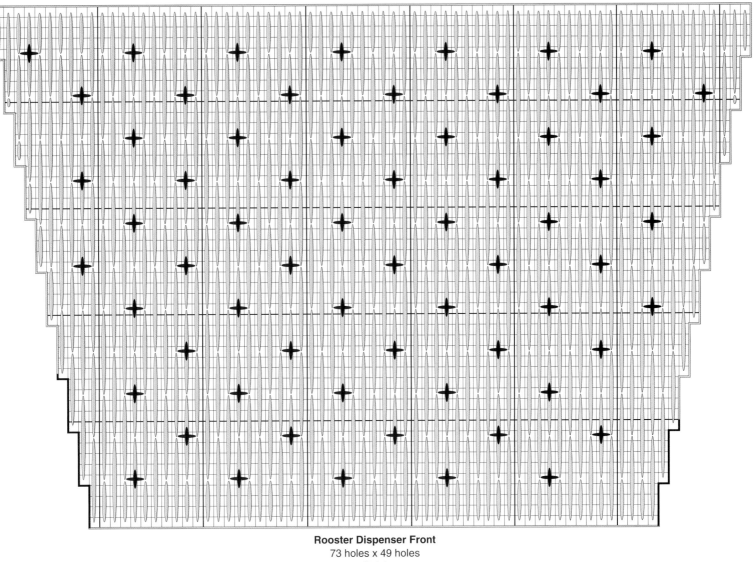

Rooster Dispenser Front
73 holes x 49 holes
Cut 1

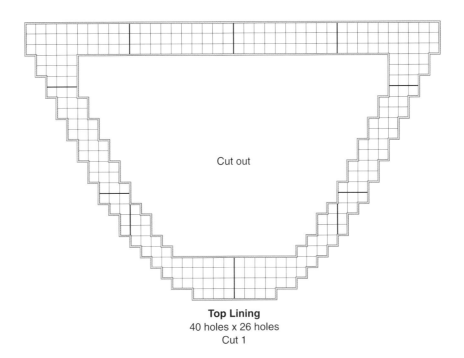

Cut out

Top Lining
40 holes x 26 holes
Cut 1

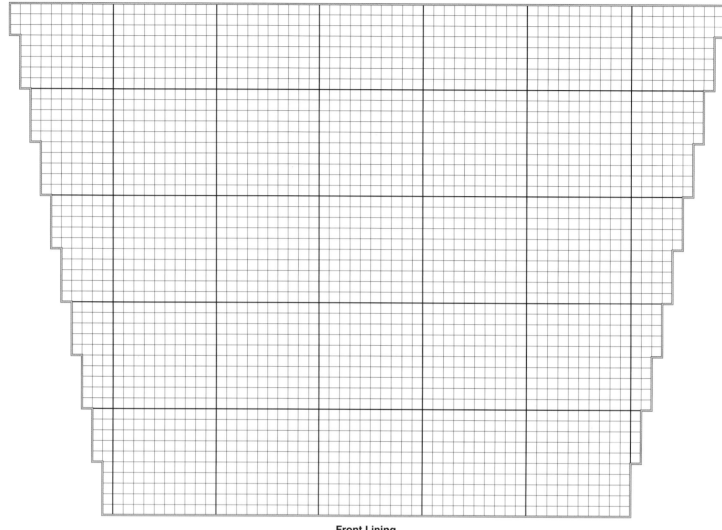

Front Lining
69 holes x 48 holes
Cut 1

COLOR KEY	
Yards	**Plastic Canvas Yarn**
30 (27.4m)	■ Black #00
160 (146.3m)	▨ Sandstone #16
	╱ Black #00 Straight Stitch
	¹/₈-Inch Metallic Ribbon
23 (21m)	■ Vintage burgundy #153V
	╱ Vintage burgundy #153V Straight Stitch
	○ Attach button

Color numbers given are for Uniek Needloft plastic canvas yarn and Kreinik ¹/₈-inch metallic ribbon.

Simply Citrus

Size: 5 inches W x 11¼ inches H x 4¼ inches D
(12.7cm x 28.6cm x 10.8cm)
Skill Level: Beginner

Materials

- ❏ 1 artist-size sheet stiff clear 7-count plastic canvas
- ❏ 2 sheets almond 7-count plastic canvas
- ❏ Uniek Needloft plastic canvas yarn as listed in color key
- ❏ Kreinik ⅛-inch (3mm) metallic ribbon as listed in color key
- ❏ 2-inch (5.1cm) gold metal ring
- ❏ #16 tapestry needle

Stitching Step by Step

Dispenser

1 From stiff clear plastic canvas, cut dispenser front according to graph. Referring to graphs on page 5, cut one dispenser top from stiff clear plastic canvas and one base from almond plastic canvas. Cut also one rectangle 33 holes x 73 holes from almond plastic canvas for back; base and back will remain unstitched.

2 Stitch top according to graph, substituting sandstone yarn for white.

3 Stitch dispenser front according to graph.

4 Using sandstone yarn, Whipstitch ring to top center edge of almond plastic canvas back so that it extends 1 inch (2.5cm) beyond top edge as shown in photo.

Lining

Referring to graphs on page 5, cut top lining and base lining from clear stiff plastic canvas. From almond plastic canvas, cut one rectangle 70 holes x 71 holes for front lining and one rectangle 29 holes x 71 holes for back lining. Lining pieces will remain unstitched.

Assembly

1 Using sandstone yarn throughout, Whipstitch side edges of front lining to side edges of back lining.

2 Whipstitch top lining to top edges and bottom lining to bottom edges to complete lining.

3 Whipstitch side edges of stitched dispenser front to side edges of dispenser back. Slide lining into dispenser.

4 Whipstitch outer curved edges of base to outer curved edges at bottom of dispenser.

5 Whipstitch inner curved edges of base and base lining together.

6 Whipstitch through all layers along back straight edges of dispenser back, base and base lining.

7 Whipstitch dispenser top to top edges. Whipstitch top and top lining together around inner opening.

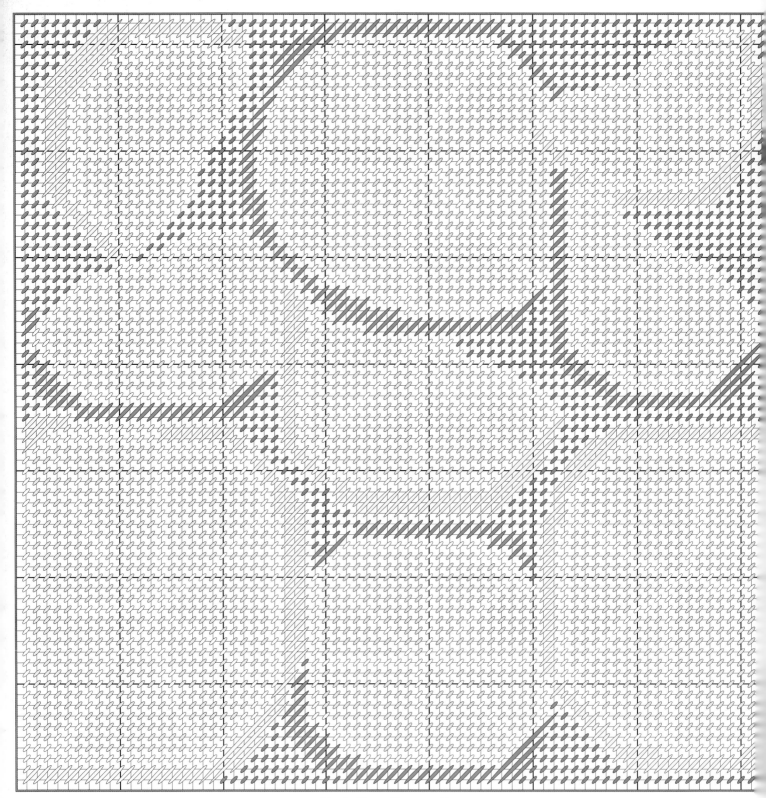

Simply Citrus Dispenser Front
73 holes x 73 holes
Cut 1 from clear stiff

COLOR KEY

Yards	Plastic Canvas Yarn
25 (22.9m)	■ Sandstone #16
15 (13.7m)	■ Christmas green #28
25 (22.9m)	☐ White #41
20 (18.3m)	☐ Yellow #57
	⅛-Inch Metallic Ribbon
60 (54.9m)	☐ Sunlight #9100
40 (36.6m)	☐ Star green #9194

Color numbers given are for Uniek Needloft plastic canvas yarn and Kreinik ⅛-inch metallic ribbon.

Butterfly Wing Bling

Size: 6¾ inches in diameter x 6⅝ inches H
(17.2cm x 16.8cm)
Skill Level: Beginner

Materials
- ❑ 1 artist-size sheet clear 7-count plastic canvas
- ❑ Scrap of black 7-count plastic canvas
- ❑ 9-inch (22.9cm) QuickShape plastic canvas circle from Uniek
- ❑ Uniek Needloft plastic canvas yarn as listed in color key
- ❑ Kreinik ⅛-inch (3mm) metallic ribbon as listed in color key
- ❑ #16 tapestry needle
- ❑ Clean, empty 34½-ounce metal coffee can with lid
- ❑ White spray paint (optional)
- ❑ Hot-glue gun

Stitching Step by Step

1 Cut one canister side and four butterfly wings from clear plastic canvas according to graphs. Cut one set of butterfly antennae from black plastic canvas according to graph. Cut one canister top from the 9-inch (22.9cm) plastic canvas circle according to graph for Beach Bounty canister top, page 9.

2 Using metallic ribbon, stitch butterfly wings on canister side according to graphs. Fill in uncoded background on canister with bright blue Continental Stitches.

3 Using black yarn, Straight Stitch butterfly bodies and antennae, stitching down bodies twice.

4 Stitch canister top according to pattern on graph using bright blue yarn.

5 *Butterfly:* Stitch wings with amethyst metallic ribbon according to graph. Hold wings together in matching pairs, wrong sides facing, and Whipstitch together along outer edges using amethyst metallic ribbon. Using black yarn throughout, Whipstitch wings together along center; Whipstitch horizontal bar of black plastic canvas antennae to top of head.

Assembly

1 Bend canister side into a ring. Using bright blue yarn throughout, Whipstitch short ends together.

2 Whipstitch canister top to upper edge of canister side; Overcast lower edge.

3 Stitch butterfly to top edge of canister as shown in photo.

Finishing

1 Spray coffee can white, if desired. Let dry.

2 Using pattern provided on page 8, cut a 4-inch (10.2cm) circle from center of plastic coffee-can lid.

3 Fill coffee can with plastic bags. Place lid on can. Slide stitched cover over can.

Joining Line
Do Not Repeat

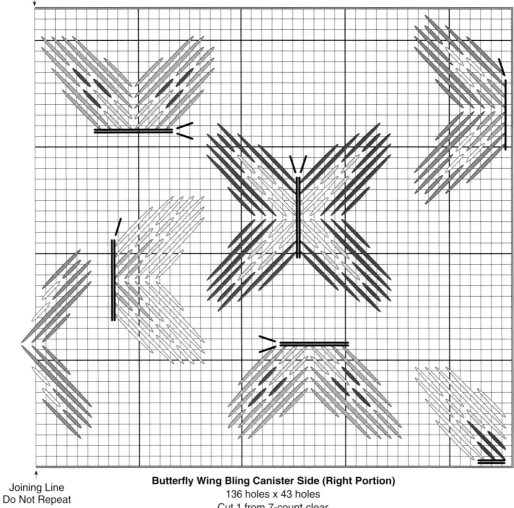

Butterfly Wing Bling Canister Side (Right Portion)
136 holes x 43 holes
Cut 1 from 7-count clear
Join with left portion before cutting as one piece

Joining Line
Do Not Repeat

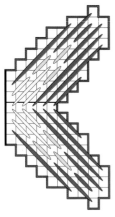

Butterfly Wing
10 holes x 19 holes
Cut 4 from 7-count clear

Antennae
2 holes x 6 holes
Cut 1 from 7-count black

COLOR KEY	
Yards	**Plastic Canvas Yarn**
100 (91.4m)	Uncoded areas are bright blue #60 Continental Stitches
5 (4.6m)	✎ Black #00 Straight Stitch and Whipstitch
	✎ Bright blue #60 Overcast and Whipstitch
	¹/₈-Inch Metallic Ribbon
9 (8.2m)	☐ Chartreuse #015
8 (7.3m)	▨ Chartreuse hi-lustre #015HL
18 (16.5m)	■ Amethyst #026
7 (6.4m)	☐ Pearl #032
10 (9.1m)	▨ Star pink #092
8 (7.3m)	☐ Sunlight #9100

Color numbers given are for Uniek Needloft plastic canvas yarn and Kreinik ¹/₈-inch metallic ribbon.

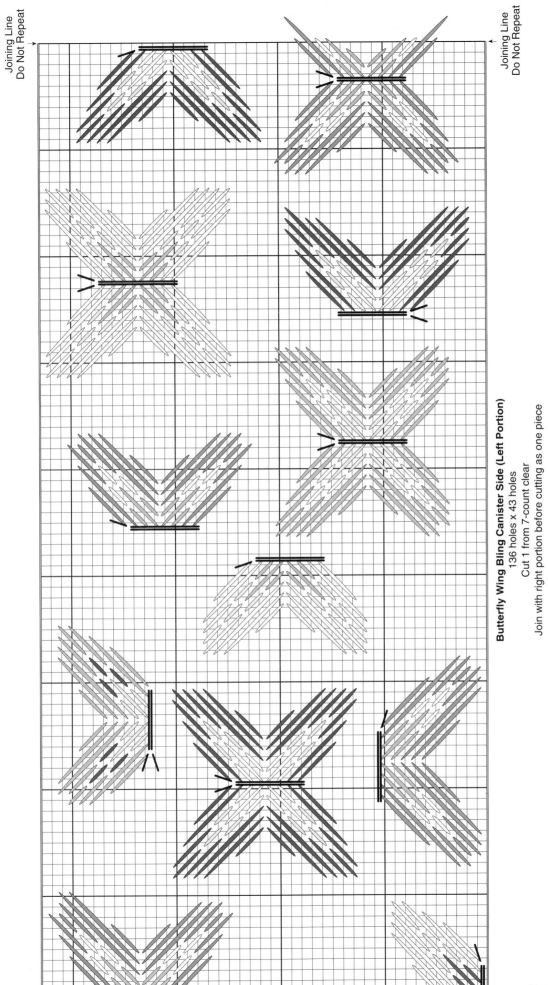

Butterfly Wing Bling Canister Side (Left Portion)
136 holes x 43 holes
Cut 1 from 7-count clear
Join with right portion before cutting as one piece

306 E. Parr Road
Berne, IN 46711
DRGnetwork.com

The full line of The Needlecraft Shop
products is carried by Annie's Attic catalog.
TOLL-FREE ORDER LINE
or to request a free catalog
(800) 582-6643
Customer Service
(800) 449-0440
Fax (800) 882-6643
Visit AnniesAttic.com

ISBN: 978-1-57367-268-9

Printed in USA

2 3 4 5 6 7 8 9

Shopping for Supplies

For supplies, first shop your local craft
and needlework stores. Some supplies
may be found in fabric, hardware and
discount stores. If you are unable to find
the supplies you need, please call Annie's
Attic at (800) 259-4000 to request a free
catalog that sells plastic canvas supplies.

Getting Started

Before You Cut

Buy one brand of canvas for each entire project, as brands can differ slightly in the distance between bars. Count holes carefully from the graph before you cut, using the bolder lines that show each 10 holes. These 10-mesh lines begin in the lower left corner of each graph to make counting easier. Mark canvas before cutting, then remove all marks completely before stitching. If the piece is cut in a rectangular or square shape and is either not worked, or worked with only one color and one type of stitch, we do not include the graph in the pattern. Instead, we give the cutting and stitching instructions in the general instructions or with the individual project instructions.

Covering the Canvas

Bring needle up from back of work, leaving a short length of yarn on back of canvas; work over short length to secure. To end a thread, weave needle and thread through the wrong side of your last few stitches; clip. Follow the numbers on the small graphs beside each stitch illustration; bring your needle up from the back of the work on odd numbers and down through the front of the work on even numbers. Work embroidery stitches last, after the canvas has been completely covered by the needlepoint stitches.

Basic Stitches

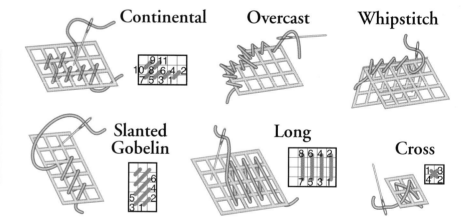

Embroidery Stitches

French Knot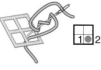

Lazy Daisy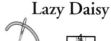

Backstitch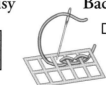

Straight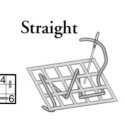

METRIC KEY:
millimeters = (mm)
centimeters = (cm)
meters = (m)
grams = (g)